CALLED TO SERVE

p. 39 Program
review

Other Books by Max De Pree:

Leadership Is an Art
Leadership Jazz
Dear Zoe
Leading without Power

CALLED TO SERVE

Creating and Nurturing
the Effective Volunteer Board

Max De Pree

William B. Eerdmans Publishing Company
Grand Rapids, Michigan / Cambridge, U.K.

Wm. B. Eerdmans Publishing Co.
255 Jefferson Ave. S.E., Grand Rapids, Michigan 49503 /
P.O. Box 163, Cambridge CB3 9PU U.K.

Printed in the United States of America

10 09 08 07 06   9 8 7 6

Library of Congress Cataloging-in-Publication Data

De Pree, Max.
     Called to serve: Creating and nurturing
the effective volunteer board / Max De Pree
          p.   cm.
     ISBN-10: 0-8028-4922-9 / ISBN-13: 978-0-8028-4922-9 (pbk.)
          1. Associations, Institutions, etc. — Management.
     2. Nonprofit organizations — Management.
     3. Boards of directors.   4. Voluntarism.   I. Title.

HV41.D28   2001
658'.048 — dc21
                                             2001033225

www.eerdmans.com

Contents

Acknowledgments

What would we do without our mentors and critics? Life would be risky. I treasure them and want to say thanks. My wife, Esther, and three of our children — Nancy, Chuck, and Jody — each active in non-profits, have made serious contributions to this book. Good friends and mentors — Paul Nelson, Tom Pratt, Shirley Showalter, and Walter Wright Jr. — offered reflections, suggestions, and corrections to the manuscript. I am most grateful for their time and insights.

Kay Vredeveld and Linda Harthorn in the essential work of typing and retyping were their usual patient, efficient, and good-humored selves. Over and over, life teaches us the beauty of interdependence. Which, of course, is what this book is all about.

Preface

This book is the result of a serious person asking the right questions. How can the board of a non-profit organization work best? Now that I'm on such a board, what should I do? How can we find the best trustees? How should I think about my work for non-profits? How can trustees contribute their best? What kind of relationship between a board and the staff will work best? How can we organize and develop the service of busy, committed people? What does their commitment entail?

There is a reason why this is a small book. We want it to be useful, but not a burden. We recognize that it's the busy people who end up on boards. They don't have time to read long books about this subject, nor do we think it's necessary. We believe good people need reminders and an occasional nudge, not a sermon. We also assume a good deal about you — that your time is valuable, that you are committed to not-for-profit work, that you, too, know something about this subject.

Several years ago, my friend Dr. Verley Sangster was invited to be the president of the Center for Urban Theological Studies in Philadelphia — CUTS. The Center is a school for adults, all of whom hold full-time jobs. It is located in a difficult urban setting. When Verley arrived to begin work, he was presented with a "club" for his steering wheel, so that his car would be less likely to be stolen. At first he thought it was a joke.

Verley first came to CUTS in 1994. In his previous position, he was Vice President of Multi-ethnic and Urban Ministries for Young Life at its headquarters in Denver, Colorado. Verley and I met when he was a student at Fuller Theological Seminary (and I, a trustee), and we have shared a two-way mentoring relationship for a good many years.

CUTS — the acronym verges on becoming a
name insiders use — is a sacred calling and a
tough challenge for all involved. CUTS was
founded in 1971. It is now an affiliate of
Geneva College in Beaver Falls, Pennsylvania,
and Westminster Theological Seminary in Glen-
side, Pennsylvania. Its students are primarily
African-American. In many ways CUTS is
unique, but in another sense it exemplifies the
more than 1½ million non-profit organizations
in America to whom this little book is addressed. It's not among the large, prominent
ones like the Salvation Army and the Red
Cross. It's different from the Boy Scouts, a local
hospital, or the town library. While it fits
broadly into a category we could call academic,
it's very different from a liberal arts college or a
major university.

Yet CUTS is one of the many non-profit organizations that are a special gift to American
society and culture. 109,000,000 Americans
work for them. The value of the time they contribute, according to a 1998 Gallup poll, is
$225.9 billion — no small sum of money. The

organizations that benefit from this energy have their own niches. They serve all kinds of people, work in all parts of the country, offer many different services, and attract their own brand of volunteers. They also share the never-ending chore of fund-raising.

Another common denominator is the need to establish and nurture governing boards that are lively, effective, fun to serve on, and demanding in the best sense of the word. The best boards combine in a fruitful way a passion for a group's mission with the competence to make a significant contribution. As you can see, I am using the word "boards" broadly in these letters. Many organizations will use a different designation.

When Verley arrived on the scene at CUTS, one thing needing his attention was the creation of just such a board. Since I had served on a number of boards over many years and since he and I work well together, we began a series of discussions about boards and life in general at non-profit organizations. I would follow up each conversation with letters for clarification and as a kind of record of our thoughts. Later I asked Verley to write his notes and suggestions on the letters. And so the two of us arrived at the beginnings of what you are reading.

Now you have the background to this book. What should you do with *Called to Serve*? Enjoy it. Try out the ideas and suggestions. Take it seriously. Don't take it too seriously. You surely can improve on it. Write in it. Put your stamp on it.

CALLED TO SERVE

Getting Started

Dear Verley,

You mentioned in one of our discussions that a major factor in your new calling was the need to develop a governing board for the study center, and you asked if I had any thoughts to share. As a matter of fact, I do. You remind me of the story about the English visitor whose hosts took him to see his first American football game. When the Americans asked him after the game what his thoughts were, he said, "The game combines the two worst elements of American culture — violence and committee meetings." Let's you and I confine ourselves to committees. We'll have to delegate violence to someone else.

With that in mind, I'm willing to try my hand at a series of letters giving you some ideas, thoughts, stories, and warnings about how to develop, nurture, grow, and reward non-profit governing boards.

I'm excited about this project, Verley. We have much to do in our discussions about boards, because over many years of working in the volunteer realm, I've come to realize that the competence of a typical volunteer board doesn't often hold a candle to the competence of the people it governs. People who work for love in volunteer organizations see important needs to be met, want to work in a values-based setting, are ready to hold themselves accountable, and expect their gifts to be properly used. In the process, while they seldom articulate it, they expect the chance to grow toward their potential. Boards can help in a remarkable way to give them that chance.

So my purpose in sending you this series of letters is to offer some ideas and to explain some ways to both leaders and followers that will liberate the gifts of volunteers especially.

Volunteer boards have the chance to enhance the lives of those who serve so many people and — why not a grand design? — American society and culture and civilization. As we begin, it's crucial to realize the astonishing uniqueness of the role of volunteers in American life. No other society has this quiet strength and vitality. We don't have to invent it, we just have to make it better.

I think you'll find as these letters unfold that this will be a dialogue of love with emphasis on building and nurturing relationships. I don't plan to propose controls and rules and structures that bind people and limit their contribution. I will not pretend to have the last word. Good people always keep on improving things when given half a chance.

Besides you and me, there is another person joining our committee. Our editor is Clark Malcolm, a writer, philosopher, pianist, and volunteer. He and I have worked together on four books. If this series of letters turns into something helpful and worthwhile, we may even prove that some committees really do do good work.

Verley, be critical (nicely, of course). Write your own notes on these letters, send Clark and me your comments. We'll do our best. The other day, Verley, as my four-year-old grandson Max was climbing into his chair, ready for his dad to cut his hair, he said, "Is your name Delilah?"

A word to the wise is sufficient. Don't ever underestimate anyone.

Warmly,
Max

▼ ▼ ▼

The Marks of an Effective Board

Dear Verley,

One way to think about a governing board is to ask ourselves "What would a really good board look like? Would we know one if we saw it in operation?" With this in mind, I'd like to suggest some marks of an effective board. No doubt you will think of others, but these will serve as a basis for some serious board building. Harking back to the English visitor watching his first football game and the committee meeting that precedes every play, one thing we can say about the game is that the participants always know the score. They know how they're doing. This is important.

I say "effective boards," because the word

"effective" sends an important signal. There's nothing wrong with efficiency (except when it becomes an excuse for avoiding the right priorities), but the chief responsibility of boards is to be effective on behalf of the organization. That's just what the organization needs from its board. Effective boards, in a nutshell, remember the long view, remember that the president and staff are human, and do the work of the board, much of which you and I can think about in later letters. Most of the work of the board takes place through the implementation of an agenda. The organization changes, the board changes, the context in which we work always changes. If the board regularly composes a well-thought-out agenda, there will always be a north star.

I once sat in on a board meeting as a visitor. Before the meeting was to begin, I asked the man next to me if I could have a look at his agenda. He said, "Oh, we don't have a real agenda. What you see is simply an exercise in random trivia." Well, that's exactly what we don't need.

Like all agendas, a board's agenda primarily implies a series of events. Effectiveness is quite a different matter. Effectiveness depends on many things, some concrete, some abstract, all having to do with relationships and commitment and competence. Having laid out a few ground rules, we can ask, what are the marks of an effective board?

An effective board has a mission statement.

▼ ▼ ▼
9

Many high-priced consultants will tell you to have the shortest possible mission statement. I don't happen to think that is such a great idea. For some organizations the shortest possible mission statement would be "Go to work." But that doesn't tell us how to behave together to be effective. A mission statement can say something about quality, about quality defined as truth. It can say something about process and diversity and orthodoxy. It can say something about those whom it seeks to serve. It can say something about how those within the organization will work toward their individual potential as well as toward the organization's potential.

I feel that the closer an organization comes to being defined as a movement, the closer it will come to fulfilling its potential. A mission statement is the place to begin to define your own movement. The more complicated the work of the group, the more talented the people involved, the more the mission statement should reflect aspects of "the movement."

At Fuller Seminary, where I serve on the board, we developed a statement called "The Mission Beyond the Mission," which suddenly enabled many people to reach a new level of literacy about what Fuller Seminary intended to be. It elaborated the mission in a useful way and helped the various parts of the Seminary understand how their own work fit into a broader vision. It also served to inform all groups about what other people were doing. In both the mission and "the mission beyond the mission," we kept in mind the important distinctions between who you intend to be and what you intend to do. In organized life, what we're able to do always results from who we intend to be.

Of course a mission ought to be feasible. It's a forlorn existence for a person or a board to be challenged to do something that's not possible. And we should remember that non-profits often turn the impossible into the improbable, and the improbable into accomplishments.

An effective board nurtures strong personal relationships.

Verley, I'll be working on a separate letter about the design of the board structure. It's an important thing, and it ought to be done well. But here I would just like to give you a warning. Many people seem to feel that a good board structure enables high performance. This is simply not so. What's crucial is the quality of our personal relationships. The chairperson and the president set the tone for good relationships, but it is up to every individual on the board to develop, nurture, and polish good relationships. I'm sure this is a theme we will develop in our conversations and in several of the letters I plan to send you. While we want to do a good job of structuring the board's work, good working relationships are more important.

An effective board stays in touch with its world (whatever its world is).

How are we to think about our world? It was interesting to me some years ago to hear the leaders of Prison Fellowship talk about their world. In some parts of the country, something like 95 percent of the people they seek to serve were black. Yet of their top 50 executives, not one was an African-American. (This has since been drastically changed.) It made for an instructive discussion about defining one's world. What is the context in which you want to work when you talk about being an effective board? How is it possible to be an effective board member if you are also an outsider?

Our world includes those we serve, where we serve, and what we do, but forces outside that world that we cannot control come into play. What constraints outside our world should guide our ideas and purposes?

I'm a great believer that management should be invited into the board's world but that the board should not go into management's area. When people are accountable for the performance of others or for the accomplishment of work, you cannot have board people supervising them. You know as well as I do, Verley, that it's difficult to serve more than one master. When the board intrudes into management's area, the board only complicates matters. The way to make sure the management of an organization is in touch with the board is to bring management to the board. For instance, when I served on the board at Hope College, a small liberal arts school, we invited the provost and the deans and the vice presidents to meet with the board and with some of its committees. We didn't send board committees into the administration's offices to discuss plans or oversee performance.

There are other ways for a board to stay in touch with its world. Herman Miller (where I served on the board for many years) is a company that does business pretty much around the globe. Herman Miller now has over 10,000 employees and, of course, a board of directors. How can the board come to understand what the company does? One way is to visit a major customer. There is no better way for a board member to learn what is going on in a corporation or a non-profit group than to spend a couple of days with a customer. It is a good education. Verley, who would you say are your customers?

An effective board does very good planning.

One of the first things for your board to do is to figure out who needs to be involved. The first question the group should ask is "What is it that we wish to be?" Then "Whom do we serve?" Next ask "What are the far-reaching implications of our planning?"

Some people need to be involved in the board's planning because they will be held accountable for results. Some people need to be involved because they have had a special experience or special knowledge about the problem;

some people need to be involved, to be blunt, because they are going to pay the bill. Planning by the board ought always to include the chief financial officer, a bringer of a necessary reality to the process. Of course, the chief financial officer should never have a role that stymies the vision. Some realities have priority over numbers.

The best boards decide whom they are going to serve, which means deciding whom they aren't going to serve. Whom does CUTS serve? To consider global implications — whether your globe includes other nations or simply other communities — is to relate a mission to geography and to social relationships. I can remember asking a very fine designer why he had designed a certain table and why he didn't want to offer that particular table base in white. He responded with a long lecture about how he had eliminated the colors he was not going to use. He hadn't *chosen* three colors; he had looked at every color available to him and decided which colors he was *not* going to use. You know, when you think about the global implications of your planning, you are ruling out the colors you are not going to use.

Another step in good planning is to define the external and internal forces at play in relation to what you are trying to do. If you have a budget of $37,000 for six months, a plan requiring $48,000 is simply unreal. Being in touch with reality is a good definition of being healthy. If you and the CUTS board aren't in touch with reality, something's wrong.

Good plans are achievable. We all know what road is paved with good intentions, and there is no faster way to perdition than a long-range plan filled with well-meaning but unrealistic intentions. A good plan is couched in achievable terms, and the actions it describes are feasible.

Good planners imagine the consequences of what they are planning. No one has the right to make a plan without creating an image of the consequences, the relationship of the consequences to the organization's mission and to the people involved. One of the wonderful things about being in business a long time is that you hear adages not taught in business school. Many contain more than a grain of wisdom. Here's one of my favorites: A good leader may never become part of the problem. Especially when the problem is a lack of foresight.

One of my goals in planning is to end up with the equivalent of a road map. It may not tell everyone exactly what roads to follow. It may not have every detail along the way. But it will help the people charged with implementing things make the right connections. It will make sure that board members and volunteers know where they are ultimately going. It will give us a sense that we are, in fact, on a journey and not simply out for a stroll.

An effective board gives itself competent and inspirational leadership.

The board depends on competent leadership. You shouldn't select leaders because they are vocal or major donors or have survived the longest or are the best politicians. Loyalty by itself is never sufficient. You always have to link loyalty and competence. One of the most unfair things in the world is to invite really good people to do simplistic work for a good cause. Another crime, it seems to me, is to give really good people poor leadership. When an organization demands true leadership and the results justify the time and energy, good boards respond with gusto.

An effective board works seriously at the growth, needs, and potential of its members.

Selection, of course, is crucial. The questions "Where do we get good people?" and "How do we get them?" are serious. The environment we create for growth and potential, as well as the satisfactions that come from doing good work well, motivate good people to work for love. I have always thought about board members as perpetual volunteers. The best of them are like lifetime free agents. Because the best board members have many opportunities and choices, the organization and its leaders develop programs for the care and feeding of these vital volunteers. They are provided good orientation and lucid, succinct information. There are ways for them to understand and become intimate with the work of the organization. They are challenged with measurable work, and maybe most important, they are thanked.

An effective board provides to the institution wisdom, wealth, work, and witness.

One of the goals for the chairperson and executive committee in selecting or assigning board members is to get at least two of these qualities from each member. That's not always easy. Failure to do so is the most forgivable when a board member brings only wealth (in abundance). It is important to point out to prospective candidates what is expected of them, including the role of active advocate. Don't hide from them what you want them to do. Don't play down what you really expect by saying, "Oh, just come aboard, it won't take a lot of work, it won't take a lot of money, etc." Misleading expectations result in nothing but grief. To tell you the truth, good people don't want to be part of something that requires little of them.

An effective board is intimate with its responsibilities.

For example, a board of trustees at a college has to understand its role in relation to the faculty, to the students, to the administration, to the various publics of the school, to the donors. While it may be difficult for a board to define these groups of people, someone on the best boards understands its constituencies. In the corporate world, when a corporation gets to a certain size and covers a certain amount of geography, there is no way to avoid having some expert in government relations. If the group is doing business in twenty-six states and filing twenty-six tax returns or selling to the federal or state governments, there must be someone who understands government. The boards of many schools, like Goshen College, for instance, benefit from access to experts on learning theory, public health education, and organizational management.

***An effective board decides what it will
measure and does it.***

A good board measures the effectiveness of its
executive team. A good board reviews the effectiveness of its members, and a good board is going to ask at the right times, "How are we doing against our plan?" A good board will always
measure the results of any major investment. A
good board will measure the appropriate inputs
as well as outputs. Failure to measure what
matters damages our future.

***An effective board plans time for
reflection.***

I remember the story, perhaps apocryphal,
about President Eisenhower and his secretary of
state, John Foster Dulles. Dulles was an inveter-
ate traveler. He seemed to be on the go continuously. At one point during the discussion of a
serious problem, President Eisenhower said to
him, "Don't just do something; stand there."
Sometimes it's easier to be busy than to take
the time to be reflective.

An effective board says "thanks."

How important it is to learn to say thank you! There are many ways to say thank you, but the problem is to find the most graceful and fitting. When I think of thanking people who have a family, I try to find a way of thanking the family — they, after all, have borne the burden of service. The right thank you doesn't have to cost a lot, but it does have to account for the needs of the people who are serving.

Verley, you remember Kareem Abdul Jabbar, one of the greatest basketball players in college and the pros for many years. Seven feet two inches tall and on his last circuit of all the towns the Lakers played in, he was honored in every city because of who he was and what he had done for basketball. In Dallas, a businessman presented a gift to Kareem and had obviously thought about saying thank you. He had a special table built, higher than usual, on which to place the gift for Kareem. The businessman observed that you shouldn't ever make a person stoop to receive a gift. Now I think that is a marvelous lesson, isn't it?

The Work of the Board

Dear Verley,

You remember our discussions about the work of the board. In other letters, we'll get into the role of the chairperson and the role of the board member, which of course are integral to the work of the board. But what are some of the things a good board actually does? What should be the board's job outline?

It seems to me the best way to look at that question is to see it through the prism of the agenda. The agenda, after all, is a kind of "right now" job outline for the board. I say right now, because time is very important in the work of a board, even though a board does not operate day to day as an administration often must.

he first thing we can say is that a board ...u its agenda ought to have a future orientation. For instance, in the life and responsibility of a board, such things as strategic plans, financial enabling and soundness, facility needs, governance, and succession plans must have a high priority. It's interesting how these are some of the various things that contribute to our legacy, which by its nature is a part of our future orientation. The board does have obligations in the short term, but the future, with certain exceptions, comes first. The board is not primarily an instrument for doing. Of course, it does some important things — but primarily the board exists for other purposes. To reflect the mission and vision and strategy of the organization, the board is responsible for determining the philosophy, the values, and the policies of the organization. You might say, as Walter Wright, formerly president of Regent College, said, "A board holds the future and mission in trust."

Certainly the board has some specific duties. Through its presence and influence, it seeks to guide the organization in its efforts toward leaving a legacy. While the administration's leadership team should be thinking through the strategic planning, the board should review and question and bring its perspective to the scrutiny of such plans.

You asked me about performance reviews. The board (or one of its committees) evaluates the work of the president or director. But the board should also review with the president an evaluation of the senior team. This gives the board advance insights into leadership succession as opportunities arise. In doing this, the board sets the example for measuring performance throughout the organization. To do its work effectively, the board, working with the management team, helps to decide priorities. It then shares in developing and maintaining a focus on these priorities, in building support, in providing resources, in overseeing the implementation and evaluating results.

The board, since it represents diverse experience and perspective, brings to the work of the organization both a strong commitment to the vision and the program of the organization, as well as an outsider's objectivity.

I have found it very helpful to think about designing an agenda by following the lines of a bell curve. At the top of the curve (that's my shorthand for the way energy at board meetings starts out slowly, then rises, then declines) for regular board meetings we will want to focus on the future and plan time to be thorough. We want to focus on our strategic plans and the outlook for their realization. We want to discuss significant issues and vexing problems. We look at these in light of what we have agreed to measure. Being disciplined about the work of the board gives its members a sense of its role and of its importance. We pay attention to key appointments and promotions because these people are our future. The selection, nurture, assignment, and evaluation of key people is the most important and most difficult task of organized work.

Let me come back to this matter of being thorough. One of the key ways in which a board behaves responsibly is by planning

enough time for members to dream together,
for members to ask questions and scrutinize together, and for members to voice contrary opinions. These opportunities should take place at
the top of the bell curve — never at the end of
the meeting. Other matters can be referred to
committees, but these are for the full board.
Think seriously about board retreats for CUTS.
I know that board members are all busy people
and that agendas are normally full to overflow-
ing, but in my experience board retreats can be
wonderfully constructive opportunities for
deepening the board members' understanding of
each other and their work together. Look for
every opportunity to be thorough.

The board's function in the areas we've been
discussing is mostly strategic and reflective.
Let's move on to areas of the work of the board
that are more tactical (even day to day at
times) and require good process. Most of this
work will be taking place with the administration or staff and with board committees. It can
be planned for on either the ascending or de-
scending leg of the bell curve.

It's important that the administration keeps the board well informed — both good and bad news — and it's important that the board allot sufficient time and attention to the work and results of the administrative team. The administrators should be diligent in sending ahead material to be read in preparation for the meeting.

A note here is in order. The chairperson should not permit anyone to read to the board. This is both a waste of time and a mark of poor preparation and therefore of inadequate respect. A board meeting is an important time together and should be used judiciously by all participants. When done well, a board meeting engages the energy of the members in what's important and eliminates the temptation of some board members to bypass the president and wander onto administrative turf.

The work of committees takes place both at the time of board meetings and between meetings. In my next letter, we'll discuss various types of committees to consider. Committees are important for at least three reasons. They have the opportunity to focus and become competent on certain matters; they serve as learning places for members when rotation is employed; they save the board time. There can be both permanent and temporary committees. Be ruthless about terminating a temporary committee when its assignment is completed.

My friend Jim Beré, who was a corporate leader, presidential advisor, and worker/advocate for many non-profits, once told me that he would serve only on boards that had hardworking executive committees. He felt it was a waste of talent and time to have the full board deal with operations matters best handled by a small committee. In the letter, I'll include for you some suggestions for the role of an executive committee. For some boards, a related agency appoints new members or strongly oversees membership. For those boards that manage their own membership, I've included suggestions for this part of their work in the letter on structure, where I talk about the role of the Trustee Affairs Committee.

Well, Verley, I hope this summarizes some of

issions on what is the work that a
tually does. Knowing you, I'm sure
you'll think of more.

▼ ▼ ▼

30

The Design of the Board Structure

Dear Verley,

We spent quite a bit of time on the work of your board, but how can you design the structure of the board? What committees should a board have? Is there a relationship between the work of the board and the selection, recruitment, and training of members? What impact does the management team have on the effectiveness of the board? What information does a board need and how does it get it?

Boards have different cultures. Their traditions and purposes vary, and so there isn't a single structure for all boards. I'm reminded of the story of two Chinese executives visiting a potential partner in a small town near Atlanta,

Georgia. Their host invited them to try a helping of grits with their breakfast. Later in the day, the always-polite Chinese men were asked how they liked the grits. After a pause to give it proper thought, one replied, "They must be very healthy." Well, our organizations are never exactly the same. Their uniquenesses are important and should be reflected in their boards. One way to think of boards is the center of a web of connections. The board is connected — or should be — to reality, to the president, and to itself. How are these connections made, maintained, and capitalized on? This is what structure is about.

A caveat: Structure is important, but what is much more important — in fact, critical — is the willingness and ability of the people involved to establish and maintain amiable and productive relationships. Whatever your reaction to my suggestions about structure, please remember it is the quality of our relationships that really counts. The structure of your board should always be thought of, first, not in terms of the work to be accomplished, but rather as an expression of what the organization intends to become. And it's too bad that many boards never realize what they're becoming. Members often come and go without ever gaining a sense that they are helping the organization become something. Inertia can be a powerful opponent.

To implement its philosophy, goals, and policies, the board appoints the director or president to whom it delegates the necessary responsibility and authority to effectively carry out the mission of the organization.

The management team plays a crucial role in making the board useful and effective and competent. We might even go so far as to say that a board can be only as good as management will help it become. An outside part-time board always depends on the administration for most of its information. While the board receives important help from outside auditors and legal counsel, and while it can do certain performance auditing on its own, it is always vulnerable to the willingness of the administrative team to enable the board to be effective.

The administrative team should always err

on the side of providing the board with too much information, rather than too little. The administrative team should never see themselves as the censors of what the board receives. The administration should be especially careful not to screen out things that may bring pain to the board. Like a good leader, a good board doesn't inflict pain; it bears pain.

An example of how the administration should deal with the board: Key proposals and issues like building programs or fund drives should always come to the board through its committees at least twice. Major decisions should not be thrust on an outside board with only one opportunity for review. There may, of course, be exceptions and emergencies, but in the life of the relationship between a board and the administration, the administration always needs to respect the fact that the board can never be as intimate with the workings of CUTS as the administration. The president must see that the administration knows this.

The board structure should be designed to

express the board's intent in three significant areas: resources, programs, and guidelines.

In resources, the board has three primary areas of interest: people (who are always the heart of the organization), financial enabling, and the physical and soft assets that the people employ. The selection, nurture, assignment, and evaluation of people should always be a primary concern. On the financial side, the finding and dispensing of money undergird the entire operation; each task demands high integrity and experienced competence. The quality and appropriateness of any asset that can have enormous effect on the way in which people achieve their objectives lie within the proper purview of the board.

From the perspective of programs, the structure of the board should be designed to signal to the organization how the board intends to monitor what the organization intends to be. Of course, what CUTS does *not* intend to be is a matter of board concern and oversight as well. The board should be a model of stewardship for the organization, a quality at the heart of volunteer work.

It is also important to formulate guidelines that bring coherence between the vision and mission of the organization and the way strategic planning is developed to reflect them. While your board should insist on a high degree of focus, it should also be giving the kind of guidance that will result in the natural fecundity of a well-run operation.

The structure of the board is expressed in its committees. Committee work is important not only because it enables the whole board to be effective, but because it serves board members who learn from a variety of committee assignments, as part of their continuing education program. Keep in mind, Verley, that committees should be designed primarily to carry out the purposes and intention of the organization and secondarily to track management's performance. Another way of saying this is that the board's work should be primarily future oriented, and to a much smaller degree, should deal with historical results. In addition, when committees do go to work, they are probably strengthening personal relationships at the same time.

Some examples of committees that may be appropriate to various organizations follow. Please keep in mind these suggestions may not meet the specific needs of CUTS. I'm sure you will give a unique character to your committee names and will define their duties in ways that vary from these models.

The **Executive Committee** acts on behalf of the board between meetings of the board in areas that are defined and restricted by the board as a whole. Its work can be organized under the three headings of Active, Advisory, and Reflective.

Active

a. Do certain work on behalf of the board between regular meetings (but do not supplant the work of the full board).
b. Evaluate the performance of the president.
c. Review the evaluations of key personnel who report directly to the president. These evaluations are done by the president but reviewed with the Executive Committee.

Advisory

a. Support and review and monitor the planning process.

b. Give counsel concerning key people
   — selection
   — opportunity
   — identity
   — development
   — equity

Reflective

a. Future oriented
b. Vision driven
c. Dedicated time for definition and analysis of major opportunities and problems
d. Dedicated time for evaluation of key programs, ideas, events, etc.

The **Finance Committee** is responsible for studying and making recommendations to the board relating to all aspects of financial planning, financial management, and financial results. It can also be the committee that reviews the organization's compensation programs and

broader matters of equity. For some orga
tions, this committee's duties could inclu
oversight of investments, endowments, and
capital programs.

The **Financial Audit Committee** is responsible for recommending to the board the appoint-
ment of outside auditors and for interacting with
the organization's auditors with respect to auditing principles and various legal matters and for
reviewing the annual audit of the organization.

All organizations have a need for an overview
of quality. Let's call this a **Program Review
Committee**. This group needs to represent your
constituencies — your students, patients, clients,
and so on. They should always keep the mission
uppermost in their minds. The objectives of a
Program Review Committee should be to (a) improve the quality of all that we do and the way
in which we do it; (b) raise the level of conscious-
ness about quality in those people responsible for
implementing programs; (c) set new or improved
organizational standards; and (d) influence the
organization without interfering.

The Program Review Committee members

should be seen as reviewers, observers, and teachers. They should be concerned with both the communication of quality and with the quality of communications. Their method of working should be to select an area for examination and to try to evaluate its effectiveness with a mix of observation and questioning. This process provides individual board members doing the auditing with an excellent way to obtain firsthand information about the organization and its effectiveness, thus making them much more informed and their contributions more valuable.

This committee should conduct reviews on its own initiative and issue reports to the president, with copies to the full board, so that reviews can take place in the normal leadership process. In one of our conversations, you thought this was a new idea worth trying.

Another very important committee that could be considered by many organizations is a **Trustee Affairs Committee**. Organizations may call this a governance committee or a board development committee. Some of the duties of this committee could be as follows:

▼ ▼ ▼

40

1. Continuously develop a list of potential board members, gather information regarding their qualifications and preparedness to serve. Prepare the nominations for consideration by the full board. (Keep in mind that four requirements of trustees are wisdom, wealth, work, and witness.) Members would ordinarily be prepared to bring at least two of these to board service.

2. Arrange and oversee the orientation and training of new board members.

3. Arrange for the full involvement of members in the activities of the board, including appropriate rotation of service among various committees.

4. Encourage members to evaluate their own performance.

5. Provide appropriate recognition for members of the board.

6. Review the vitality and effectiveness and appropriateness of the board's functioning and make recommendations for change.

A special area of opportunity for Trustee Affairs Committees these days is the opportunity to deal with diversity. Here I am talking about two kinds of diversity. The committee should make sure that the board has the variety of expertise it needs to deal with the broad spectrum of its responsibilities. The other area of diversity is at least as important — a diversity of people on the board. We are seeing more and more women and members of minorities represented on volunteer boards and agencies, a wonderful thing. Their presence is not sufficient; board members must be ready to listen. I believe that volunteer boards can increase this kind of diversity — as they should — and demonstrate the patent advantages of hearing the insights and wisdom women and members of minorities bring from their experience and can offer the board.

Some organizations may need committees on facilities. Other organizations, such as an educational institution, would probably want committees on academic affairs, student affairs, faculty matters, and fund-raising. In some cases where the organization is very complex, a committee on resource management could well be in order.

There are surely times in the life of organizations when temporary committees or work teams need to be formed, do their work, and then be disbanded. Structure should never be seen as something precious. It should always be seen as a tool or a vehicle and subject to change to meet the needs of the organization and especially the needs of the people serving on the board. Always keep in mind, Verley, that people, not structures, change the world.

▾ ▾ ▾

43

The Role of the Chairperson

Dear Verley,

Perhaps the most crucial element in turning a group of volunteers into an effective organization is the perception the chairperson has of her role and the way that she carries out her responsibilities. One way to think about this is to see the chairperson's role as a needs-meeting job. Just as the organization and its clients have needs to be met, so does the board itself. With this in mind, I'll review a number of qualities board members have a right to look for in their chairperson, qualities your board should expect in its chairperson. Keep in mind that most of these are matters that the chairperson is uniquely positioned to deal with. A chairperson cannot dodge her responsibilities. She must come to the job with the time and flexibility to shoulder her duties.

Believe it or not, I have to remind you that the chairperson chairs a board meeting, not a president or senior staff person. They are important resource persons, but the chairperson chairs. She gives leadership to the devotional bond-making in the group. She manages the board's time. She maintains appropriate focus. Not everything, as you know, carries equal weight. She senses mood and response. She calls the rest and toilet breaks every group needs. She monitors the discussions and at the appropriate time calls for the vote. (Remember, the chairperson votes only in case of a tie.) It often is not enough simply to vote on an action or a direction. It is up to the chairperson to follow action with assignment and to set a timetable for reporting back to the board.

She works continuously at developing her skills in leading meetings, trying always to give each member the opportunity to participate and guarding against the temptation to speak too frequently herself. Bob Greenleaf, whom we've talked about before, taught me the advantages of a chairperson's occasionally declaring periods of silence in meetings for reflection, for absorbing conflicting opinions, for respecting an entirely new idea. I highly recommend it.

In many, perhaps most, organizations there is a president, a pastor, a conductor, or other full-time staff. The chairperson makes it her business to establish a strong covenant with that person. She commits to his success. She makes time to be available. They work together in designing the agenda and reviewing the board's effectiveness. They work out together who speaks for the institution. There are usually a variety of publics to be considered when the institution communicates on matters of vision, mission, values, and strategy. It should always be clear to the members who speaks for them.

I served for a number of years as chairperson of the board of Fuller Theological Seminary in Pasadena, California. Dr. David Hubbard, the president, and I would, of course, find time to talk together when the board met. In addition, we often met for a day at the Denver airport, halfway for both of us. We reserved a room in the United Airlines Red Carpet Lounge and could work together four or five hours and still be home that evening. These were very fruitful times.

The chairperson is probably the key person when it comes to building trust in the group. Oddly, one of the best ways to build trust is to be sure to share bad news. Of course, there are other things we do to build trust, such as giving plenty of opportunity to ask questions and to scrutinize proposals. Good communicators build trust. Keeping promises builds trust. Respecting everyone equally builds trust.

The chairperson is the one who enables and draws out the members. She gains the contribution of all, either in session or out, never allowing anyone to be isolated. She is an aggressive listener and asks the kind of questions that lead to productive answers. She is skilled at guiding the movement away from personal agendas and focusing always on the corporate agenda. She makes it her business to know what's fragile in the group and deals sensitively with these matters (I've got a letter planned to discuss the inevitable tensions among board members).

Another role of the chairperson is to make available an orientation and education program for new members. They need to know the institutional issues, its history and traditions, its past citizens and giants. New members must identify with the institution's mission, values, and strategies. I believe the best way to work at this is to assign each new member an experienced member as a mentor. This is especially true in the case of people with little or no previous experience on boards because of age, gender, or ethnic background. They can then sit together at board meetings, and they should plan on talking together on the phone and even visiting together in between meetings of the board. This is a wonderful way to orient and involve new members.

It's also important to think about continuing education for the board as a body. One of

the important things that Dr. Hubbard did was
to arrange institutional forums at Fuller. He
would bring the faculty and the board of trustees together for these forums, where we all had
the opportunity to interact with the speaker
and sit together in small groups to discuss the
presentations. These were wonderful learning
opportunities. Dr. Hubbard often arranged
these forums in three ways. At times, he would
have a key and influential person speak to us,
such as Richard Ostling, the religion editor of
Time magazine. At other times, he invited critics of the seminary's program and theology. At
other times, he invited what I would call teachers, such as Michael Novak and Earl Palmer, to
speak to and interact with the group.

Verley, I'd like to close this letter with two
admonitions. The first is that the chairperson
must be diligent in saying thank you. The second is that the chairperson must be just as diligent in holding the group accountable. By the
nature of the chairperson's position, no one else
in the group can hold the board accountable if
she fails to do it. In other letters, I've talked

about deciding what to measure, and this is the way in which the chairperson holds the group accountable — by whether or not the group measures up to the goals and standards they have set for themselves.

What Does a Trustee Promise?

Dear Verley,

The opportunity to be a member of a non-profit board is a special gift to us as persons seeking to serve and grow. It is also a special gift from us to society through the legion of organizations that are vehicles for the missions and passions and visions that make us a civilization. Seen in this light, membership on a governing board should never be taken lightly or accepted merely as an honor. It is a responsible, demanding job.

In our discussions we asked ourselves several questions about the role of a trustee. How can we envision this job? How can we think about our potential contribution to the organization?

How should we interact with others on this board? How will I know if I am doing a good job? Let's begin with what it means to take trusteeship seriously. Like other forms of leadership, it's not a position or an honor, but rather a demanding responsibility, a meddling in other people's lives, and hard work that requires continuous learning. There is always a need for serious preparation and a commitment to serve when we accept leadership responsibilities.

▾ ▾ ▾

54

One of the ways in which we can take our trusteeship seriously is through faithfulness and commitment to the organization and what it stands for. If the organization has a mission statement or a statement of faith, we should be able to understand it, accept it, and advocate it. We will, of course, want to sign on to the organization's values. In our efforts to be accountable, we get to the meetings. We arrive on time and prepared. We do our work. Understanding the importance of signals to others, we make our gifts, and we speak a good word on its behalf. These seem like simple things, Verley, but they are easily forgotten.

Next, it seems to me, a trustee should decide what to promise. What are your special gifts? What uniqueness in this diverse group is yours? In what ways is the opportunity to serve on this board a special opportunity? What are the needs of this organization that you can effectively deal with or help with? When one deals with the two questions "Who am I in this context?" and "What is my purpose?" then you can formulate the promises you are ready to make.

Third, a trustee needs to establish strong covenantal relationships. These are the secret to effectiveness in group activity. Covenantal relationships are vastly different from contracts. They deal in shared beliefs, shared values, shared commitments, and shared promises. Covenantal relationships exhibit a love and commitment together in the pursuit of our mission. It means that we spend reflective time together; that we're vulnerable to each other; that we can challenge each other in love and deal with conflicts as mature adults.

One of our goals should be a devotional

▼ ▼ ▼

bonding that enables enormous accomplishment and growth together. This approach to
working together is not limited to the board
members, but is shared broadly with others involved in the activity of the group — the staff,
students, donors, clients, families, whoever they
may be.

*A trustee should become an institutional advo-
cate.* This, of course, requires a deep understanding of the organization and its mission. It
does not require complete agreement with all of
the ways in which things are done. It requires
rather a mature acceptance of differences and
practices. All of us accept and do many things
in life as adults without necessarily agreeing
with them. This is one of the secrets of successful groups. Advocacy requires us to be committed to the institution and committed to the
success of the leader of the board. Advocates
need to be passionate and, of course, competent. One without the other never works very
well.

Being an advocate requires one to be productive. Remember our friend David Hubbard used

to say that he always looked for the three Ws in prospective board persons: work, wisdom, and wealth. My friend Phil Miller, a fellow board member with me at Hope College, added the fourth W — witness. Let's always aim for three but insist on two. Given the financial pressures most non-profit organizations are under, we do occasionally make an exception for the truly wealthy individual who's willing to support us.

Advocates need to be prepared to live with some pain. In board work, there are always financial surprises, disappointments in people, uncomfortable confrontations, and goals not met. True advocates not only learn to live with some pain, but they also learn to bear the pain of others.

This brings us to one of our most challenging discussions. *A trustee should work to establish pertinent and compassionate ways to measure what matters.* How can we evaluate the performance of people on boards who are basically volunteers, who work for love? They don't have to be here; they serve without compensation; they can't normally be fired. While there ought to be understandings that call attention to the need for measuring our performance, and while it's helpful to have a trustee affairs committee to ensure this can happen, evaluation is such a ticklish matter with volunteers that I have come to be a great believer in the need for written reflections as a way of gauging service and contribution.

As a member of the Board of Fuller Theological Seminary, to gain a perspective on my service to the board, I liked to ponder questions like these: Who will be honest with me? Do I bring health to this organization? Am I keeping the promises I made? Am I in sync personally with the stated mission of the Seminary? Am I informed enough to make knowledgeable decisions? Are our board meetings effective? Does the Seminary communicate regularly and effectively with me? Am I adequately informed about the Seminary's work so that I can become a spokesperson? Do I contribute adequately to capital campaigns? While these questions are oriented toward the Seminary, I believe the general elements can be broadly applied to other non-profit boards.

As the last element in the role of the trustee, let me suggest a few personal guidelines. For instance, please don't try to manage. This is the job of the president you have retained, and you have delegated that to her. Be a frantic learner. Feel a strong obligation to learn everything you can about your organization's history, about its vision, its mission, its present circumstances, and the people in it.

Learn how to separate your self (that is, your ego) from the issue. Understand that just your presence is not enough for your organization. Be prepared to give and to raise money. Keep in mind the "ethical chain" that binds you together in your mission. Work at building trust, telling the truth, serving the needs of clients, explaining the vision, and growing in the process.

As you know, each person will put her own slant on playing the role of trustee. That is how it should be. That's why I can only give you guidelines; there are very few hard and fast

rules. Yet it seems to me that of all the roles to
be played in a non-profit group, that of trustee
is especially difficult. It requires us to keep a
certain perspective and balance many things —
present and future, person and institution,
those who serve and those who are served. It is
also a role so vitally necessary that we owe it
to our common good to work at it.

▼ ▼ ▼

A Chairperson's Guide

Dear Verley,

Let's take a look at some guidelines for a chair-person. To do this, we begin by thinking of the needs of board members. One important need and a source of renewal on any board is the rotation of chairpersons. We should always set a time of service for the chairperson. A person could, for instance, serve two 2-year terms and then give up the chair to someone else. To fail to rotate the chairperson on a regular schedule is a matter of great risk to any board. What we are discussing in this letter is also for folks who will have their crack at being chairperson in the future. Chairing is where servant leadership comes strongly into play.

In reviewing for a moment the needs of participants, you and I can look to our own experience. Most people have a need to serve and to be given the opportunity to contribute to something that has meaning and worth. We're not asking for easy jobs — we intend to work and be stretched. We need to be taken seriously, which is always the first sign of respect. In the process, we would like our lives to be enriched, and we need a chance to reach toward our potential. We may never know what our potential is, but the search for that mystery is exciting. Our leaders get the chance to share the journey.

The things we agreed on are relatively simple and are based on years of experience. I've organized these thoughts and suggestions under six headings. Observing these guidelines will make service more effective, more fun, more efficient, and certainly more rewarding. It will increase our respect for our organization and for our own worth and contribution. These guidelines are not magic — just common sense — but they must be put into practice. Since the chairperson's job is at heart a matter of stewardship, she continually asks herself two questions: What do I owe this group, and what matters?

Build Community

Building community starts with devotional bonding. People who work for love are devoted — devoted to beliefs, principles, values, clients, goals, etc. Discussing our devotedness openly and together builds community. We strengthen that community by recognizing and meeting the needs of the followers. What do followers need from leaders in achieving organizational and personal goals, and what are their needs for the future? We also build community when together we are successful; so the chairperson focuses on enabling (that is, drawing out) the contribution of each member. He serves the group's needs rather than his own. The practice of hospitality also builds community, but I'll get to that later.

Design the Agenda

You and I should emphasize the word "design," because a purposeful, thoughtful agenda contributes significantly to a group's effectiveness. We can't get by with just making a list. In thinking about designing an agenda, we include a review of all plans and assignments. We try to lead the group in focusing on goals, opportunities, and problems. Surprises are always difficult to deal with, so we try hard not to let them happen.

The chairperson is a big help to the group when she makes sure her own ego needs (as well as those of the members) are kept separate from the issues. It helps here to be good at clarifying reality.

By the way, one of the great time wasters for any group is the routine of giving progress reports when there's been no progress. The chair should check, while designing the agenda, with subcommittee chairpersons to ensure there will be substance to their reports. If not, don't risk frustrating the commitment of good people.

Use the Bell Curve

One way to present a well-designed agenda is to follow the bell curve. This best reflects how boards and committees actually behave. For instance, some folks, like it or not, come late and some leave early. Socially we're inclined to require a settling-in time, during which we get used to being together again and need a period of easy work. This is the left side of the bell.

▾ ▾ ▾

Then we're ready to get down to business. Now we are approaching our most productive time as a group. We're wide awake, we have good energy. This is when we tackle the heavy stuff. Everybody is there, we have good focus. As we move over the top of the bell, we deal with our most significant matters. One of the sins that many leaders commit is to hold important or troublesome matters until the end of the meeting; yet exactly these matters ought to be considered at the top of the bell curve when the group's energy is at its best.

Now that we've given it our best shot, we move down the right side of the bell. We do some fun stuff. We tell our stories. Those who leave early get their chance. We wind down to the final very important item.

Verley, let me tell you a story. Several weeks ago, I received in the mail a letter addressed "Max De Pree, Author of Dear Zoe, Holland, Michigan" and on the bottom of the envelope was a note in red that said, "Please, God, help get this letter to him." Well, I was astonished that the post office had gone to the trouble of finding where that ought to be delivered, so I called the post office because I wanted to thank the postmaster for what they had done. When a man at the post office answered the phone, he said the postmaster was in a meeting, and I said, "Fine. I'll call back later." And then he said, "If it's a problem, I can take care of it." And I said, "No, it's not a problem. I just want to say thank you." "Oh," he said, "I'll get him out of the meeting." And he did; so I told the postmaster the story and thanked him for the special service, and at that point, he really surprised me. He said, "We find about 100 letters like this a week that we have to do some spe-

▾ ▾ ▾

66

cial work on to get them delivered. You're the first person who ever called to say thank you."

While you will think of other ways of nurturing the board, never neglect to recognize, celebrate, and say thanks.

Be a Good Communicator

Being in touch with the members in a variety of ways contributes mightily to the effectiveness of the board. Lavish is a good word to ponder. It would be difficult to communicate too much.

The way to start is to be sure to send the agenda well ahead of the meetings. This eliminates excuses for arriving unprepared. A friend told me recently that when he gets his agenda package only a day or two before the meeting, he knows he is not being taken seriously. It's important to gain the contribution of all members. Occasionally we can have folks who seldom speak during the meeting. This does not mean they have nothing to say. It means rather that the chairperson should invite their thoughts in other ways.

I'd like to caution against withholding difficult-to-deal-with information or bad news. It's often more important to share bad news than good news. Especially in a setting where there is full-time management, the board should never be kept in the dark. It is up to the management to enable the board with all appropriate information. Another way to communicate is by producing usable minutes of the meeting in a short time. Here are some suggestions about minutes.

Minutes always need a heading that includes the organization's name, date, time, and place of the meeting.

- State who of the group are in attendance, who are missing, and who presides.
- Make sure that the following are recorded, but always be concise: reports, actions, proposals, discussions, referrals, assignments.
- Record that the meeting was adjourned.
- The secretary signs the minutes.

- Distribute to all members as soon as possible.

Practice Hospitality

As a chairperson, you are probably thinking, "Of course I'm hospitable," and I don't doubt it, but let me just put down a few reminders.

Hospitality has to do with equity for each member. Enabling each to feel authentic and needed and worthwhile is an act of hospitality. In groups of people who work for love, hospitality is an expression of civility. The way we provide for the needs of the group in the physical setting is a part of this. For instance, the arrangement of chairs and tables, the quality of the light, the tastefulness of the room demand your attention. Asking people to sit in a circle with no table is surely a distracting and ineffective way to work, as is putting people at a long, narrow table where they can have contact with only those adjacent to them. Think about the tools we need — our pads and pens; our copies of agenda, minutes, records, and reports; and where we're to put them. Think, too, about the social needs. Things go better with snacks, drinks, timely breaks, and no anxiety as to where the toilets are — small matters that should never become distractions.

Hold the Group Accountable

One of the key responsibilities of any leader is to hold the group accountable. We decide what we're going to do; that is, what outcomes are needed. This is one of the things (you'll think of more) we measure. We maintain our focus (not everything carries equal weight). We manage our time. We scrutinize our progress, our work patterns, and our results. We never ignore the need to be effective and accountable. We never let talk become a substitute for action; our goal is not to leave the board meeting with a blank piece of paper. We live by our own rules: if we have established terms for board membership, we enforce them. If we're not observing our own rules, we change them. This is a matter of equity and integrity and sets an example for other volunteers.

Well, Verley, these are some thoughts concerning guidelines for chairpersons and for those who will be chairpersons in the future. It's interesting how much of this is just horse sense and how most of it is relational rather than technical.

▼ ▼ ▼

Living with Tensions

Dear Verley,

One of the myths of volunteer board work is
that you see only fine, well-motivated people
who agree on what needs to be done, when to
do it, and how to do it. Nothing could be further from reality. Any diligent board suffers certain tensions. Perhaps this letter should be la-
beled "dire warnings." Good people disagree, do
a little politicking, try to make decisions in the
bathroom (the worst form of exclusion), and
come to meetings totally unprepared.

I'm not about to promise you that these
folks can be changed. Conflict resolution begins
with an awareness of the central problems and
an openness to dialogue before the lid pops.

One of my favorite high school teachers loved to admonish us, "A word to the wise is sufficient." Let me review a few "words to the wise."

We should probably start with a very legitimate tension: tradition versus change. Some folks honestly believe change is our only hope. Others feel that we build our future by honoring our past. You'll find this is a tough one to balance. It's very much related to the need to deal constructively with constraints. Often people think that with a few more resources, their problems will disappear. Of course this is not true. Few of us ever have all the resources we wish for. Our job is to help board members see that constraints are a fact of life. They are — believe me — along with reasoned restraint, one of the secrets to outstanding performance. Constraints perceived and understood are especially valuable to the creative processes that feed our strategic thinking. In fact, Charles Eames, perhaps the most famous industrial designer of this century, often said that constraints are liberating.

Another thing to keep your eye on, Verley, is the difficulty some folks have perceiving and accepting new realities. Things change. Our working environment changes. We change. Matters beyond our control affect us. Opportunities arise; sometimes too many. Getting your group to have a broad perspective at the same time they keep their priorities in focus is no mean feat. But if you know it's normal, you'll be ready to deal with it.

▾ ▾ ▾

Tensions predictably arise when an organization or its board confronts a crisis. Perhaps the crisis is financial, perhaps it is brought about by the resignation of an especially important board member or president, perhaps a management problem creates a crisis. Sometimes tensions develop into a crisis: the president is not performing; the budget goes into the red; a focus on finance pushes everything else into the background; the organization is bleeding and boring board members. Crises call for new attention to the purpose of the group and the quality of human relationships, both of which are key to success and faithfulness. When a board finds itself in crisis, it becomes a sin to sit on your hands and hope it will go away. Get to work!

One of the more tendentious matters to arise — seemingly, often, out of thin air — is the need for a leader to move on to another position. Although in retrospect the signals are clear, at the time it is difficult to know when a president or conductor should be preparing the organization for someone else to take over. If he isn't taking the initiative, the board must step in. No one stays forever. Changes in leadership are refreshing, not the end of the world. We simply face reality. Maybe it's simply time to retire.

Occasionally there is malfeasance. More often, the pace slows, the vision blurs, people make mistakes, weariness sets in and life for followers and constituents becomes difficult. Ineffectiveness moves in like a virus. It's time for a change. Not only does the board's decision about what to do have to be scrupulously right, but the way in which the board implements the change has to be as clear and as obvious to everybody as the reasons to change. Once again, hope by itself will not be sufficient.

In the letter on the role of trustees, I reviewed some ideas on the matter of evaluating a board member's performance. This is guaranteed to produce tension. Most boards and committees I know won't touch it with a ten-foot pole. I can understand that. Suggesting that a volunteer be evaluated seems a little crass, and it probably is — unless we're serious about our mission, unless we truly believe members want to grow and reach their potential and serve society, unless we take our clients seriously, unless we respect our donors. Maybe we ought to be ready to deal with this tension. Good practice indicates we should discuss this with prospective members, so that they are not surprised.

Which brings us to another tension. While lovers may love good surprises and can usually deal with bad ones, it's asking too much of a diverse group to handle bad surprises well. An example is when a committee preempts a full board responsibility and moves ahead on its

▾ ▾ ▾

77

own. A board may be organic, but it is not the same as an individual whose reactions may be predictable. We are diverse and therefore very different as persons. In the process of reaching consensus and making decisions, we each have "different straws that break the camel's back." Boards don't deal well with surprise.

Another tension arises when board members try to move onto management's turf. Sometimes good members do this without intending to. It's up to the chairperson to keep an eye on this. The board has assigned the supervision of staff to the president; and the staff deserves only one boss.

Another tension arises when new members, unaware of decisions made by their predecessors, change board policy and direction when this may not be the best thing to do. This is an area where good staff work can keep the board out of trouble and prevent problems.

The last item I'd like to mention is the tension that arises when the board tries to deal with its own contribution and value to the organization. Deciding what we will measure, de-

ciding who matters and what matters, determining the quality of our service and product
— these are not easy things to confront, even
though in theory we all agree on their importance.

For a starter, Verley, these are some dire
warnings. I guess the fact that board work is so
important may be what makes it such a cher-
ished and satisfying challenge.

▼ ▼ ▼

79

What the Board Owes the President

Dear Verley,

In doing seminars on this board business over the years, people have often been surprised by my insistence that we talk about what the board owes the president (or the conductor, or the pastor, or the manager). Since what has seemed to me to be both natural and transparent often comes as a surprise, let's review this idea. I see four categories of things the board owes the president: mandate, trust, space, and care.

Mandate

The mandate for a non-profit leader should include a number of non-mysterious elements, unequivocally stated, understood by everyone. (Remember, we are committed to communicate lavishly.) A mandate always begins with a clear statement of who we intend to be. What we do is always a consequence of who we intend to be. Our mandate should always include a mission statement and a strategy, both of which derive clearly from who we intend to be. Naturally we must examine our purposes carefully before we decide who we intend to be. Our commitments to clients, volunteers and staff, donors, and the public will all depend from these three over-arching elements — our intentions, our mission, and our strategy.

The next elements of the president's mandate are the statement of expectation and a definition of what will be measured in his performance institutionally, professionally, and personally. Some folks like the idea of a job outline. For leaders, I much prefer a statement of expectations. A job outline can become a kind of box that tends to limit the leader's imagination. We surely don't want that.

A marvelously productive freedom can result from the way in which we link the statement of expectations to the promise of what will be measured. There should be no ambiguity here. Promising what will be measured institutionally, professionally, and personally promises sincerity about the opportunity for the president to reach his potential along with the organization.

Years ago, one of my mentors, George Nelson, the wonderfully original writer and industrial designer, warned me to learn to listen more carefully after someone uses the word "but." When we think about the mandate to the president and how we charge him, there are three things to keep in mind. First, we deliver the mandate without any "buts." Second, we commit to sharing in the job of maintaining the organization's focus. Third, we bluntly express our support by promising and showing that we are committed to his success.

Trust

In much of our thinking and talking about how organizations work, the power of one word is regularly underestimated — trust. Trust is an enormous treasure for any organization. The board surely owes this to its president or conductor, just as he surely owes it to the entire organization. Trust doesn't arrive in our possession easily or cheaply, nor does it guarantee to stay around. It can slip away unnoticed by inattentive leaders. Trust is easier for me to understand if I consider its elements. Trust requires respect — which means we take every person seriously. Trust multiplies with truth — without adjectives and not subject to redefinition by cornered leaders. Trust requires moral purpose, as well as keeping our promises. Demonstrating competence and making the nobler choice are part of how followers judge the character of leaders and whether to award them their trust. When leaders fail to see their obligation to be the initiators of reconciliation, trust begins to wane.

So, Verley, this is a quick review of the trust the board owes the president. If you wish to think more about the role of trust (and I hope you don't conclude that I'm just trying to make another sale!), there's a whole chapter on it in my book *Leading Without Power*.

Space

Like everyone else, the leader of an organization needs space, in the context of this letter, space to become president. This, too, the board owes. My good friend and mentor, Dr. Carl Frost, has taught a good many of us that when we are promoted to president, it does not mean we are instantly qualified. The board and the organization are actually giving us only, as Carl would put it, "the opportunity to become president" — a great chance, but still only a chance. Whether or not we make it is partly up to us and partly up to other factors, especially the insights, efforts, and commitment of those who gave us the opportunity.

One of the ways a board gives space is by establishing a workable structure, which we've already talked about. The board also gives a president space by acting with him to set the priorities, as well as working to involve the entire organization in understanding and adopting those priorities. How can a board expect a president to paint a coherent or imaginative picture on an unlimited canvas?

Another way for the board to create space for a president is to play a "review and reflect" role in the selection, nurture, assignment, and evaluation of key people. Developing key people is probably the most important and most difficult part of a leader's job, and he needs all the help he can get. The board's role in reflection is very special. Please check my comments on this in the letter on structure, specifically the role of an executive committee.

There are two further elements to providing space. It is wonderful for the organization's future when the board takes a strong interest in opportunities given the president for personal growth and when the board makes it clear that it expects the president to hold the entire organization accountable for realizing its mission and strategy. In the rush of the day to day, a president often neglects his own growth; the board can issue a friendly reminder every once in a while. Likewise, a mission and strategy often lose immediacy in the daily work of a group. A board should surely reflect with a president on the mission and strategy, why they exist and should be consulted often.

▾ ▾ ▾

87

Care

The fourth thing the board owes the president is care. I mean care in several senses: the kind of care that arises from the devotional bonding I wrote about earlier; the kind of care that recognizes the needs of a president's family for friendship, support, and love; the kind of care that makes both vacations and regular health checkups mandatory; the kind of care that goes the extra mile in compensation arrangements to include such things as budgeted spouse travel allowance and financial planning service; the kind of care that sees the president's need for continuing education and development — especially the opportunity to be mentored — as crucial to the organization's future; and finally, the kind of care that keeps the president alive, that doesn't permit him to "work himself to death."

So let's keep in mind that the board owes all of this to the president. It is a gift to know clearly what is expected; it is not a chore. It is a light on the president's path.

Here's a kind of a grace note, Verley. When we think about the board's relationship with its designated leader, there's a nuance at play that I think we shouldn't forget. What we plan to do differs enormously from what we leave behind. A strategic plan is a long-term commitment to something we intend to do. A legacy, on the other hand, is the facts of our behavior that remain in the minds of others, the cumulative, informal record of how close we came to the person we intended to be.

Last Things

Dear Verley,

We've come to the end of our list of topics. I
hope that you haven't found my ramblings te-
dious or too detailed. It's just that my experience has convinced me that no detail is too
small to consider carefully when it comes to
thinking about the important work of non-
profit boards and the people who serve on
them. Now I'd like to end with a story.

My brother Hugh is 85 years old. Most of
his career was spent with Herman Miller, Inc.,
where for 17 years he served as CEO. This was
a very significant time of innovation and
growth in the company's history, and he did an
outstanding job.

Upon retiring, he moved to Florida and became involved in a number of activities in the Naples area, the most significant of which is his service on the Board of the Naples Philharmonic Symphony, including a couple of significant building programs.

Like others who have served on many boards in their lifetime, Hugh came to the point in his life where he had had enough of boards (with the exception of the Symphony Board, on which he continues to sit). He wanted to do something where he was personally more directly involved. So he joined Habitat for Humanity, a wonderfully constructive organization. For a number of years he has found great satisfaction in helping build homes for people who drastically need them. At one point during one of our conversations, he mentioned that he was reconsidering his calling to Habitat for Humanity because they had changed the rules. When I asked him what that was all about, he said, "Well, they have passed a new rule that says people who are over 80 years old may no longer work on the roof." What really bothered

Hugh was that the organization had not consulted any of the eighty-year-olds about the change. After giving some thought to his story, and after we had chuckled over his chagrin, he reached the conclusion that it was a reasonable new rule and he was ready to abide by it.

There's a lesson here for all of us engaged in volunteer activities. Be careful not to give people too many reasons for reconsidering their calling. Consider deeply and meticulously why it is that so many people are called to serve others as volunteers. Never forget that non-profit work, like no other endeavor, engages our choice, our hearts, and our spirits.